$14.50   28402

DATE DUE

09.06

The Gateway Arch

Places in American History

by Frances E. Ruffin

Reading consultant: Susan Nations, M.Ed., author/literacy coach/consultant in literacy development

WEEKLY WR READER®
EARLY LEARNING LIBRARY

Please visit our web site at: www.earlyliteracy.cc
For a free color catalog describing Weekly Reader® Early Learning Library's
list of high-quality books, call 1-877-445-5824 (USA) or 1-800-387-3178 (Canada).
Weekly Reader® Early Learning Library's fax: (414) 336-0164.

Library of Congress Cataloging-in-Publication Data

Ruffin, Frances E.
    The Gateway Arch / by Frances E. Ruffin.
       p. cm. — (Places in American history)
    Includes bibliographical references and index.
    ISBN 0-8368-6409-3 (lib. bdg.)
    ISBN 0-8368-6416-6 (softcover)
    1. Gateway Arch (Saint Louis, Mo)—Juvenile literature. 2. Arches—Missouri—Saint Louis—
Design and construction—Juvenile literature. I. Title.
  TA660.A7R84   2006
  725.'960977866—dc22   2005026269

This edition first published in 2006 by
Weekly Reader® Early Learning Library
A Member of the WRC Media Family of Companies
330 West Olive Street, Suite 100
Milwaukee, WI 53212 USA

Managing Editor: Valerie J. Weber
Editor: Barbara Kiely Miller
Art direction: Tammy West
Graphic design: Dave Kowalski
Photo research: Diane Laska-Swanke

Photo credits: Cover, title, © James P. Rowan; pp. 4, 7, 8, 9, 11, 12, 13, 14, 15, 16, 17, 18, 19,
20, 21 Jefferson National Expansion Memorial/National Park Service; p. 5 © Hulton Archive/
Getty Images; p. 6 Dave Kowalski/© Weekly Reader Early Learning Library, 2006

Printed in the United States of America

1 2 3 4 5 6 7 8 9 10 09 08 07 06

Table of Contents

The Gateway Arch stands between the Mississippi River and St. Louis's Old Courthouse.

Honoring Thomas Jefferson

The Gateway Arch is the tallest monument in the United States. Monuments remind us about important people and events. The arch was built along the banks of the Mississippi River. It stands high above the city of St. Louis, Missouri. It represents the gateway, or entry, to the western United States.

The Gateway Arch was built to honor President Thomas Jefferson. In 1803, President Jefferson bought land in North America from France. Native Americans had lived on the land for thousands of years, but France had claimed it. The purchase of this land was called the Louisiana Purchase. The new land made the United States twice as big.

Thomas Jefferson was the nation's third president. He served from 1801 to 1809.

Lewis and Clark reached the Pacific Ocean in November 1805.

Louisiana Purchase
Louis and Clark Expedition
Outward Route ----
Return Route (two parties) ----

St. Louis

Mississippi River

The Gateway Arch also honors Meriwether Lewis and William Clark. In 1804, the two men set out on a trip from St. Louis. They were looking for a way to travel to the Pacific Ocean by boat. They met many Native Americans who helped them on their trip. The two explorers drew maps of the rivers in the western United States. Their maps helped people find new homes in the West.

A Winning Idea

In 1935, a group of leaders in St. Louis wanted to build a national monument in the city. They held a contest to find the best idea. Two hundred people entered the contest. Eero Saarinen, an architect, won.

Architect Eero Saarinen designed the Gateway Arch. His first design had three legs.

7

By 1939, buildings in St. Louis crowded the edge of the Mississippi River. The buildings on thirty-six blocks had to be removed to make room for the arch.

Saarinen's idea was to build a simple arch. The arch would stand for the growth of the country and its western pioneers. On February 12, 1963, work on the Gateway Arch began.

Solving Problems

The idea of the arch looked simple on paper. It would be a tall arc, a curve of stainless steel. Before the builders started work, however, they had to solve some problems.

Before the arch was built, architect Eero Saarinen drew a picture of it surrounded by a park.

The two legs of the arch would be 630 feet (192 meters) apart at the bottom. The top of the arch would be 630 feet (192 m) tall.

Tall Structures in the World

Name of Structure	Location	Total Height	
		Feet	Meters
Taipei 101 Tower	Taipei, Taiwan	1,671	509
Sears Tower	Chicago	1,450	442
Eiffel Tower	Paris, France	985	300
Gateway Arch	St. Louis	630	192
Washington Monument	Washington, D.C.	555	169
Statue of Liberty	New York	305	93

The builders had to be very exact. All the builders'
work had to be perfect. The arch's two legs had to
curve and meet at the top.

Special tracks on the outside of each leg carried building
materials up the arch.

Building the Arch

The builders dug deep holes for the foundation, or bottom, of each leg. Each hole had to be about 45 feet (14 m) deep. The builders blasted through dirt and rock to finish the holes. They filled the foundation holes with concrete. The bottoms of the foundations rest on solid bedrock.

The builders poured concrete both below and above the ground to make the legs of the arch strong.

To make the arch, workers stacked steel blocks shaped like triangles on top of each other. The largest blocks were placed at the bottom. The smallest were placed at the top. The huge blocks were hollow on the inside. Smooth stainless steel covered the arch outside.

The arch is made from 142 steel blocks. Each block is joined to the next by steel bands.

Building the arch was dangerous work, but no
workers were killed.

The men who built the arch were often in danger.
They worried about the wind. High winds could
blow workers right off the arch. High winds could
also make the legs swing and crash to the ground.

Each leg of the arch had to support its own weight. It also had to support more than 80 tons (73 tonnes) of workers and equipment.

The Gateway Arch weighs 17,246 tons (15,645 tonnes). The distance between the bottom of each leg is longer than two football fields.

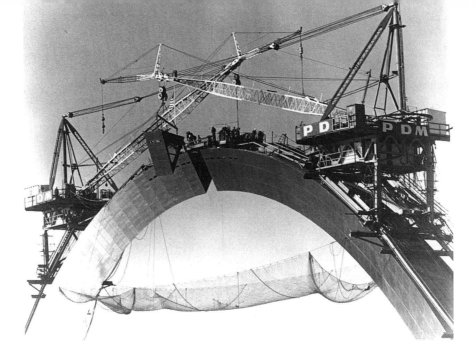

In 1965, workers carefully fit the last piece of the
arch into place.

The Gateway Arch was completed on October 28,
1965. Building the arch took less than two years.
The arch used more stainless steel than any other
building project.

Visiting the Arch

More than one million people visit the Gateway
Arch every year. Many take an exciting tram ride to
the top of the arch. The trams are like little trains
with eight small cars. Each car holds five people.
One tram travels up inside each leg of the arch.

The doors for the tram cars are only 4 and one-half feet
(1 and one-third meters) high.

The trip to the top of the arch takes four minutes. At the top, people can get out of the tram to look at the view. On a clear day, people can see for 30 miles (48 kilometers).

Each day, 6,400 visitors can ride to the top of the arch. They can look out the small windows to see the view.

The Museum of Westward Expansion sits below the arch. Pictures of people line its walls. One wall shows Native Americans who lived on the Great Plains. Other walls show pioneers, soldiers, buffalo hunters, and farmers.

Museum visitors can learn about Native people who lived in the western United States.

Pioneers on the Great Plains cut chunks of earth
and grass from the ground. They used this sod to
build their houses.

The museum shows how people lived in the West.
A Native American tepee, or tent, is on display.
Visitors can also see a pioneer's sod house. Other
displays show mounted, or stuffed, animals that
once lived in great numbers in the West. They
include a buffalo, beavers, and a horse.

The Gateway Arch stands at the start of the country's western frontier. Both the arch and the museum remind everyone how our new nation grew.

The Gateway Arch is a shining symbol of America's westward movement.

Glossary

architect — a person who draws plans for buildings and other structures

bedrock — the solid rock that is beneath the soil and other material on the surface of Earth

expansion — the opening up or the widening of something

foundation — the part of a building that is below ground and that is used to support the building

frontier — a remote area where people do not usually live

Great Plains — a large area of land east of the Rocky Mountains that runs from Canada to Texas

monument — a sculpture or building made to honor and remember important people or events

pioneers – people who are among the first to settle in a place

stainless steel — a material made from a mixture of steel and other metals; it does not rust

For More Information

Books

Gateway Arch. All Aboard America (series). Julie Murray (ABDO Publishing)

Lewis and Clark. History Makers BIOS (series). Candice R. Ransom (Lerner Publishing)

Lewis and Clark. Raintree Biographies (series). Mary Stout (Raintree)

Thomas Jefferson and the Louisiana Purchase. Westward Ho! (series). Emily Raabe (PowerKids Press)

Web Sites

Go West across America with Lewis & Clark

www.nationalgeographic.com/west
Pretend to be a member of Lewis and Clark's trip across the West and make the decisions these explorers faced.

St. Louis Gateway Arch US Symbols

www.enchantedlearning.com/history/us/monuments/stlouisarch
Information about the design and building of the Arch

Index

About the Author

Frances E. Ruffin has written more than twenty-four books for children. She enjoys reading and writing about the lives of famous and ordinary people. She lives in New York City with her son, Timothy, a young writer who is writing his first novel.